KT-439-930

FUN PROJECTS -FOR- KIDS

Vivienne Bolton

p

This is a Parragon Book
This edition published in 2002

Parragon
Queen Street House
4 Queen Street
Bath BA1 1HE, UK

9780752584010

Produced by Miles Kelly Publishing Ltd
This edition and cover design by Design Principals, Warminster

Copyright © Parragon 1998

All rights reserved. No part of this publication may be reproduced,
stored in a retrieval system, or transmitted by any means, electronic,
mechanical, photocopying, recording, or otherwise, without the prior
permission of the copyright holder.

A copy of the British Library Cataloguing-in-Publication Data
is available from the British Library.

ISBN 0-75258-401-4

Printed in China

Contents

Pot Pourri

To make your own pot pourri you will first need to gather a selection of fragrant petals and dry them in a warm, airy spot away from direct sunlight. Roses and lavender are both very sweet smelling and can easily be grown in a town or country garden. A handful of rose petals can be dried in a paper bag hung up in an airy spot and small bunches of lavender flowers can be hung up on a line to dry naturally in the air. Once you have dried your petals you will be able to mix up some pot pourri. You could place bowls of pot pourri around a room to make it smell of summer or make some lacy bags to contain small quantities of pot pourri to keep your drawers and clothes sweet smelling.

1 To dry rose petals you will need to place them in a warm airy spot away from direct sunlight. If you don't have the space to leave things out put a few petals in a paper bag and hang it up in an airy place. Choose some roses or other flowers which are sweet smelling. Check with an adult before you pick any flowers from the garden.

2 Besides petals you can dry orange and lemon peel, whole small flowers and some leaves. Spices can also be added to dried petals to enhance the perfume of the pot pourri. Cinnamon and mixed spice, cloves and nutmeg can all be put in pot pourri. If you don't have a flower garden to pick from, you may be able to purchase dried petals from your local wholefood shop. You could ask at the florist for any discarded flowers and buds.

4 One way of making good use of pot pourri is to tie it in lace or muslin bags to place in your drawers and cupboards. They will make your clothes smell sweet and some petals and leaves will discourage moths and other unwanted insects from living among your clothes. When, after some weeks the scent fades, fill the bags with newly made pot pourri.

Pot Pourri:

1 cup of fragrant dried rose petals and rosebuds

Half a cup of dried lavender petals

1 cinnamon stick, broken up

A large pinch of cloves

Dried orange peel, broken up

1 teaspoon of sea salt

Mix all the ingredients together in a bowl

You will need:

Dried rose petals and rosebuds

Dried lavender

Selection of dried fragrant leaves and petals

Bowl

Cinnamon sticks

Lace, muslin and ribbon

Needle and thread

AUTUMN LEAVES
Leaf Pictures

In autumn the leaves on the trees turn from green to brown and all sorts of golden red colours in between. When you are out on an autumn walk collect some leaves of varying shapes, sizes and colours. At home, press them between the pages of a book. Choose the colours carefully and make sure the leaves you choose don't have tears or holes. When they are dry they still show some of their colour. You can then use them as bookmarks on their own and maybe save the best ones to frame as a picture, to hang on a wall, as a reminder of autumn. Try sponging the leaves with gold paint for a good effect.

1 To make a leaf picture choose leaves that have a good shape and colour, and are not torn or broken. Carefully place them between the pages of a book and leave for several weeks to flatten and dry.

4 When the black paint is dry, give the leaves an antique metallic look by using a dry sponge with some gold paint. Don't cover the whole leaf with gold paint, make it patchy and interesting.

2 When the leaves are ready, arrange them on a sheet of paper. When you are happy with the picture use glue to hold them in place. Put your picture into a frame.

5 When the gold paint is dry the leaves are ready to be placed in a frame. It may be an idea to collect a selection of leaves from a favourite walk. Press and gild them and when they are framed you can give the picture a title and sign it.

3 In this project the leaf pictures are made more decorative with gold paint, sponged over the leaves. Before you apply the gold, cover the leaves with a layer of black paint.

You will need:

Autumn leaves

Glue

Picture frame

Paint-brush

Black paint

Gold paint

Sponge

Saucer

Desert Gardens

Growing a desert garden can be most rewarding. Garden centres and florists stock cactus plants. It is a good idea to check what plants are available before you buy a suitable planter. You will need a sunny windowsill on which to place your planted desert garden. Choose a pot large enough to hold a few cacti so that the overall impression is of a small corner of the desert. When you have planted the cacti, decorate the scene with some stones to resemble boulders.

You will need:

Plant pot

Gravel

Old spoon or small garden trowel

Cactus potting compost

Cactus plants

Suitable gloves

Selection of stones and crytals

White sand

1 Begin by placing a layer of gravel. This will provide drainage for the plants.

2 Next add a good layer of suitable cactus potting compost. Press it down firmly.

3 Dig small holes in the compost and plant the cacti. Remember to wear gloves.

4 Create a realistic-looking desert scene with some attractive stones and crystals.

5 When you are happy with the look of your desert garden, cover the compost with a layer of white sand. This will give the impression of desert sand.

Cactus plants need special growing conditions. Keep them hot in summer; place the desert garden on a windowsill that gets sunlight most of the day. Water your plants sparingly and regularly.

Always wear thick gloves when handling cacti as the spines and prickles are sharp.

Dough Baskets

Use salt and flour dough to make a basket for bread rolls or fruit. Once baked in the oven the basket is ready for you to paint and varnish. Flower shapes or dough fruit make very good decoration. Use animal-shaped biscuit cutters to make dough pets with the leftover dough. Always bake the pieces thoroughly and allow them to get quite cold before you paint them.

Salt and flour dough is not good to eat, keep it away from young brothers and sisters.

Always wash out your paint and varnish brushes, keep them clean and ready to use.

You will need:

Wooden spoon and large bowl

2 cups of flour

1 cup of salt

1 cup of water

A little spare flour

Rolling pin

Knife

Shallow oven-proof dish

Aluminium foil to line your dish

Acrylic paint and brushes

Water-based varnish

1 Use a wooden spoon to mix the flour, salt and water well. When it forms a ball take it out of the bowl and knead it for 5 minutes. Sprinkle some flour onto the worksurface to prevent the dough sticking as you work.

2 When the dough is smooth roll it out onto a floured surface and cut it into strips about 2 cm wide.

3 Cover a bowl with aluminium foil. Weave the strips into the bowl. Make the cherries from small balls of dough.
Use a short piece of thin wire or two small sticks for the cherry stalks.

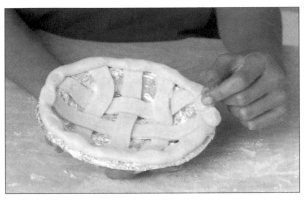

4 Bake the basket for 4 hours at 130°C, gas mark 1 to 2 or until it is completely dry.

5 When your model is cool take it out of the bowl, paint and varnish.

Fabric Printing

Decorate a traycloth or table napkins with apple or carrot prints. The prints are made using real fruit and vegetables cut in half. Green peppers make good prints too. Fabric paints come in plenty of colours and are easy to use – follow the directions written on the container. Always try your design out on a piece of scrap paper before you print on the fabric to test out how much fabric paint you need.

Protect your worksurface with newspaper before you begin. Keep some kitchen towel handy in case of spills.

If you cannot get hold of fabric paint, try using acrylic paint. You will not be able to wash the cloth but it will make a great wall hanging for the kitchen.

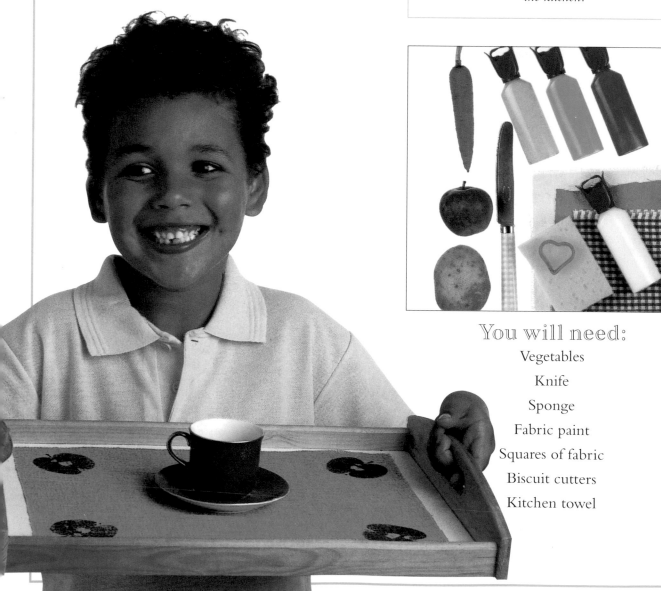

You will need:

Vegetables

Knife

Sponge

Fabric paint

Squares of fabric

Biscuit cutters

Kitchen towel

1 Cut a carrot in half. Use a sponge to spread a little fabric paint onto the carrot half. Gently press it down onto the fabric. Only press once and do not move it about when you press. Print a row of carrots on the cloth. Leave the printed cloth in a safe place to dry. Follow the directions that come with the fabric paint to set the dye.

2 Cut a potato in half. Press the biscuit cutter firmly into the flesh of the potato. Use a knife to carefully cut away the excess potato. Remove the biscuit cutter and you have a stamp ready for printing. Pat the stamp dry with some kitchen towel. Use a sponge to apply the fabric paint to the potato cut and print your pattern.

3 Halved apples printed on this green table mat look jolly. You will need to pat the cut surface dry with a piece of kitchen towel. Use the sponge to apply red fabric paint to the apple surface and press firmly down onto the green table mats.

Glass Painting

Glass painting is a great hobby and a good way of recycling empty jam jars and bottles or personalising glasses to give away as gifts or use in the home. Glass paints also work well on plastic containers, so collect a few large plastic containers and decorate them for use in the kitchen, for storing dried pasta or beans. Glass paints come in a wide variety of colours and are easy to use. Experiment with simple designs at first. Always try out your ideas on paper before painting on glass. If you make a mistake on the glass wipe the paint off quickly and start again.

1 Before you begin wash and dry the glass. Use the black outliner to mark up the pattern. Be sure there are no gaps for the glass paint to escape through. When the black outliner is completely dry use a dry brush to dip into the glass paint. Wash the brush well between colours and dry it before dipping it into the next colour.

2 Use the gold outliner on its own for this stylish look. Think about what will be in the container when deciding on colour and design.

3 Save tiny jars to decorate and fill with jam.

You will need:

Selection of glasses, jars and bottles

Outliners in black, gold and silver

Paint-brush

Water-soluble glass paints

Kitchen towel for spills

Remember to protect your work surface with newspaper before you begin.

Always make sure the glasses and jars are washed and dried with a clean cloth before you begin to decorate them.

Candy Cushions

Dyed with wax crayons, these cushions will look soft and cuddly on your bed or on the playroom sofa. The cushions are made with calico fabric and are easy shapes to cut out and decorate. The wax crayon patterns can be ironed on to set them firmly. You could make a whole bag of candy cushions for your bed. A calico cat or doll would be great fun to decorate with wax crayons.

You will need:

Calico fabric

Wax crayons

Scissors

Needle and thread

Polyester stuffing

Brown paper

1 Fold the fabric in half to make a double layer. Draw a large wrapped candy shape on the calico.

3 Cut out the cushion shapes and turn them right sides in. Sew together leaving a gap for the stuffing.

2 Use the wax crayons to colour the candy shape in swirls and dots, making it as realistic as possible.

4 Turn right side out. At this stage you should ask an adult to help iron the cushion shape between brown paper to seal the dye. Stuff the cushion with polyester.

RECYCLED PLASTIC
Mobiles

Recycle milk and juice containers and turn them into colourful mobiles. The sleepy sheep would look good above your bed and the stars and flowers could hang in a sunny window. The mobiles are painted using water-soluble glass paints and outliners. If you don't have those to hand you can use coloured, permanent markers instead to create a similar effect.

You will need:

Florist's wire

Small pliers

Flat sided plastic milk or drink carton

Scissors

Outliner

Paint-brushes

Water-soluble glass paints

Needle

Gold thread

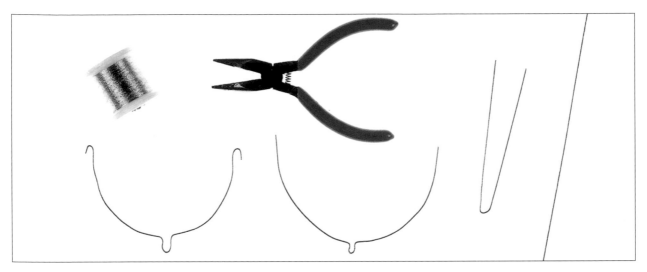

1 Florist's wire is easy to bend, start with a 20cm length. Begin by folding it in half. Then use the pliers to shape the mobile hanger and hooks. You will need three hangers for each mobile and each hanger should be exactly the same shape and size.

2 Use the scissors to cut the plastic container into suitable shapes for decoration. Wash the shapes and dry with a clean cloth. Outline the design and when the outliner is hard use a dry brush and glass paint to colour the shape.

3 Assemble the mobile by making a hole with the needle through the shapes and threading the gold thread through. Hang up the shapes and your mobile is complete.

Letter Rack

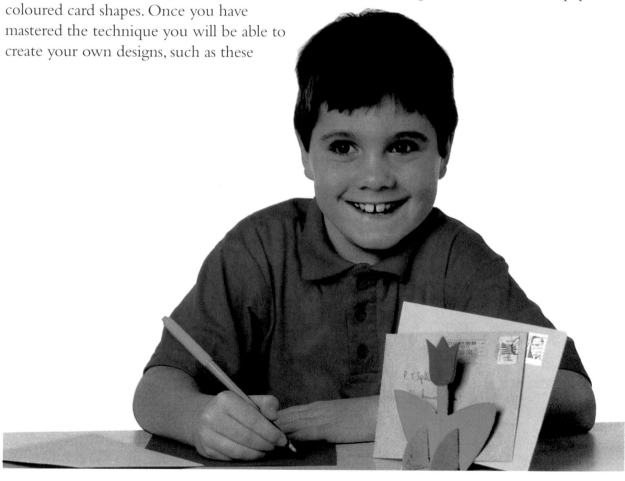

K eep your mail in check with these bright red tulips! The letter rack is made by slotting together thick coloured card shapes. Once you have mastered the technique you will be able to create your own designs, such as these flower patterns or maybe have a go at the ship at sea. The ship is a little more detailed, with the design cut from coloured paper.

1 Draw the design on thick, coloured card. The green bases will need to be cut straight to stand level on the table. The flowerheads are cut from coloured paper. Cut all the pieces out.

2 Colour the plain side of the card with crayons. Slot the letter rack together. You may need to make a rough one first to get the shape and slots right.

The letter rack can be made of card cut from a cereal packet or from a grocery box. You may need to cover the pieces of card with a layer of papier mâché to make them more sturdy and create a good surface to paint or colour.

3 Glue on the flower heads and your letter rack is ready to hold the mail.

You will need:
Thick coloured card

Scissors

Coloured paper

Crayons

Glue

Concertina Cards

Make one of these cards and watch the concertina movement when you open and close the card. The clown gives a good impression of playing his concertina, and the ballerina's tutu stands proudly out. The poodle's ruff looks almost real! The cards are quite simple to make, so think up some ideas of your own. You could use the concertina shape to make a bumble bee's body, or maybe a wriggly worm holding an umbrella! Use a little imagination and some brightly coloured paper to create a novel concertina card for a friend's birthday.

1 Fold a sheet of paper in half to form the card. Use the ruler to measure where to fix the concertina ends. Mark the two points, which should be evenly spaced on either side of the central fold.

4 You will need to cut a long narrow strip of yellow paper to make the concertina. Fold it to form a fan. When folding paper always use your thumbnail to press the fold firmly down.

2 Draw the clown with the arms ending at the dots. Make the picture quite simple.

5 Use glue to attach each end of the concertina to the end of the clown's arms.

3 Colour in your picture with bright shades, making it as attractive as possible.

You will need:

Paper

Ruler

Felt tip pens

Scissors

Glue

PAPER AND RIBBON
Gift Bags

Pack your Christmas gifts in these brightly coloured paper bags. You can make them almost any size. Use one layer of paper for smaller bags and a double layer to make larger bags. You could decorate the paper before you begin. Make a stencil to decorate the paper if you are making a lot of bags all to match for party favours. The bag handles can be made from string or pretty ribbon. Have a look around for paper decorated on both sides, or use gold or silver paper.

You will need:
A selection of paper

Glue

Hole punch

Ribbon

1 Begin by folding the paper in by about one quarter of its length. Run your thumbnail along the fold to mark it well.

2 Turn the folded sheet of paper over and apply glue to one end.

3 Glue the edges together to form a cylinder shape. Allow the glue to dry.

4 Flatten the cylinder shape. Run your thumbnail along the edges to make a good fold.

5 Fold about one quarter over on each side.

6 Open the two folds and press them inwards. You should now have a bag shape.

7 Make a fold upwards to form the base of the bag. Glue it down.

8 Use a hole punch to make holes to thread a ribbon through and make a handle.

Cut-out Cards

Make a row of paper flowerpots and turn them into a birthday card, or a row of blue and white teapots to send as an invitation to tea. The Christmas tree cards can be decorated as brightly as you wish and the colourful fish swimming around in their bowls will brighten up the mantlepiece. Cut-out cards are quick and easy to make and decorate. When choosing the shape remember that the card will need to be cut out so draw a compact picture. A Christmas tree cut from plain white paper and decorated using a gold pen would be very stylish.

You will need:

Paper

Felt tip pens

Crayons

Scissors

Glue

Sequins to decorate

When decorating your cards try outlining coloured-in pictures with a darker shade. This will accentuate the shapes and give the cards a professional finish.

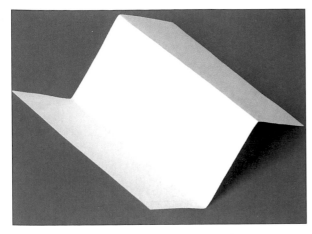

1 This card is easy to make and fun to colour, you will need a rectangle of plain white paper. Fold the sheet of paper in three to make the card shape

4 Colour in your card using bright shades.

2 On the front of the card draw a pot of flowers. Make sure the flower pots are joined at the lip, or the card will fall apart when you cut it out.

5 To make this cheery Christmas card use a sheet of green paper folded in three. Draw on the Christmas tree shape and cut it out. Take care to leave the branches joined together at the base of the tree. Glue on small flowerpots cut from paper for the trees to stand in and decorate the Christmas trees with sequins and shiny stars, glued on.

3 Cut away the excess paper.

Photo Album

S easide holidays are best remembered in photographs. Make one of these albums to keep your photographs safe. Choose bright nautical colours; blue and yellow are fun. The albums are made from card and coloured cord holds the pages together. Try making a seaside collage to decorate the cover. A beach scene or a gaily coloured yacht would look good.

You will need:
Thin coloured card

Coloured paper

Scissors

Hole punch

Cord

1 Cut the covers and pages to size. Use the hole punch to make holes through the covers and pages. You will need to take care that they line up. Thread coloured cord through the holes to hold the album together securely and tie a bow.

2 To make the photograph holders cut a narrow strip of paper. Fold the paper inwards to create a corner sleeve. Cut away any excess paper and glue the sleeve onto the page. Do this four times, one for each corner then insert the photograph.

3 Decorate the cover of your album with an attractive seaside collage. Use coloured paper to create this yacht and cut out a row of waves to glue along the bottom of the page.

Seaside Jewellery

Shells, attractive stones and small pieces of driftwood can be made up into earrings and pendants. Use fine wire and thread to assemble the jewellery. You can also buy ready-made clasps and earring backs from craft shops. These are called jewellery findings. Look along the seashore for two matching shells with small holes in and make them up into earrings. As you walk along the beach keep an eye out for interestingly shaped, coloured stones.

You will need:

Pebbles and shells

Wire

Thread

Jewellery findings

Varnish

Paint-brush

1 These dainty shell earrings are easy to make. These shells have tiny holes naturally occurring in them. However you may have to use a press-together jewelry binding to hold the shell in place. Attach the earring hook to each shell and you have a pretty pair of earrings to wear as a reminder of your seaside visit.

2 To make these pendants you will need some attractively marked pebbles. Use clear varnish painted over the pebbles to bring out the rich patterns (clear nail varnish works just as well).

Wind a piece of wire around the pebble and finish with a loop at the top. Attach a piece of thread to the loop and use this to hang your pendant around your neck.

Check that it is okay to pick up shells along the beach where you are.

PAINTED PEBBLES
Paperweights

Pebble painting is fun and a good rainy day activity. Collect pebbles along the beach and save them. When you want to enjoy a quiet time get out the paints and your imagination, and make these attractive paperweights. You could paint a tiny row of pebble cottages (use a fine paint-brush to paint on tiny windows and doors) and little rose bushes along the cottage front. Or try your hand at painting a tiny kitten on a pebble or a fish or even a skeleton.

1 These interesting decorations need a little time and practice. Wash and dry the pebbles before you begin. Use a fine paint-brush to paint in the detail. Once you are happy with your chosen decoration and the paint has dried, add a layer of varnish.

2 A row of painted pebble cottages makes a good ornamental display. Choose pebbles which have suitable shapes and which can stand up. You may need to apply two coats of paint to the house and roof to give a good surface for decorating. When you have painted the cottages give them a coat of varnish to protect them and to give them a glossy finish.

You will need:
Pebbles
Paint, varnish and paint-brushes

Blow Football

Football is a very popular sport. Enjoy a game of blow football on a rainy day by making your own table sized football pitch. This pitch has been made with a piece of sponge board. If you wanted to make a more long lasting pitch, you could get an adult to help prepare a piece of chipboard or plywood. You will also need green felt to cover the board although paint would give a reasonable surface. The game is played using drinking straws and table tennis balls. Each player begins with an equal number of balls and sees how many he or she can blow into the opposite goal. Once you become more professional, you might want to play a more traditional football game with one ball decorated using a marker pen to look like a real football.

You will need:

Sponge board

Green felt

Scissors

Glue

Shaped craft strip wood

Paint

Paint-brushes

Cocktail sticks

Coloured paper

A shoebox

Drinking straws

Table tennis balls

1 Cut out the felt slightly larger than the board. Spread the board with glue and press the felt onto the board.

2 Cut the edging to size and paint it yellow. As well as both sides and ends of the pitch, you will need four small pieces to make the corners.

3 Glue the edging in place and use the white paint to mark out the goal mouths and centre line.

4 Press a cocktail stick into each corner of your pitch. Fold the coloured paper in half and cut out four flag shapes. Glue the flags onto the cocktail sticks.

5 Cut the shoebox in half. Paint the halves white and when they are dry place them on the pitch at opposite goal mouths. Put the table tennis balls in position and it's time to challenge someone to a game!

CARDBOARD
Toy Cars

These cute little cars are great fun to make and given a push will whizz along a smooth surface. The wheels are made from milk or juice container lids, cocktail sticks and straws. The car chassis is cut from either coloured card or the sides of a recycled grocery box.

You will need:

Thick card

Scissors

Masking tape

Paint

Paint-brushes

Four juice or milk carton lids

Straws

Cocktail sticks

1 Begin by drawing two side views of a car. Cut them out. Next cut out a long rectangular shape. The width of the rectangle decides how wide the car is.

2 Use the scissors to cut out two small v-shapes to form the wheel arches. The wheel axles will run through these v-shapes. The wheel axles will be held in place by the base of the car.

3 Now you are ready to assemble your car. Use masking tape to attach the long rectangular shape to the car sides. Do this and you will see the car take shape.

4 Cut a piece of card to fit in the base of the car. Tape it in place. Your car is now ready to paint and decorate. You could paint on a family sitting in the car.

5 To make the wheels each lid will need a hole made through its centre. Push the end of a straw through the hole. Now use a cocktail stick to hold it in place. Break the ends off so that the wheel turns.

6 Push the wheel axle all the way through and attach the second wheel. Cut off any long pieces of straw to fit the car. Now make and fit the second axle.

GREEN LENTILS AND FABRIC
Juggling Balls

Juggling is a great skill to develop. It takes time and patience but can be most fulfilling. Make yourself some juggling balls and a set for a friend and practise together. These juggling balls are made from printed cotton fabric and filled with uncooked green lentils. Lentils are a perfect filling as they will give the juggling balls some weight and be easy to grip. They are also quite economically priced – and – if you stop juggling you can cook the lentils for supper!

1 Cut a rectangle of fabric and fold it in half. Sew seams along the side edges. Sew strong stitches close together or ask an adult for help and use a sewing machine.

2 Turn the bag shape right side out.

3 Half fill the bags with green lentils.

Juggling balls would make a great birthday gift for a friend.

4 Close the bag making a triangular shape by bringing the two side seam ends together and neatly fold the edges inside to allow for the final seam.

5 Sew the edge together firmly.

You will need:

Fabric

Scissors

Green lentils

Needle and thread

RECYCLED CONTAINERS
Money Boxes

These stylishly decorated money boxes would look good in the living room. They are made from recycled containers which have good, well-fitting lids. Encourage the whole family to make savings by decorating money boxes for them all. Flowers painted pink, bright orange and yellow, or a money box that suits a particular hobby or style – you can create them easily from old boxes.

You will need:

Sturdy containers with well-fitting lids

Scissors

Newspaper

Glue

Paint

Paint-brushes

1 You will need an adult to help you cut out the money slit. Use a large coin to help measure the space.

3 When the papier mâché is dry, paint on the base colour, then paint on tiny trees and shrubs.

2 Glue squares of newspaper onto the box to make a good painting surface.

4 These money boxes are made from cardboard boxes. Cut out a slit before covering completely with papier mâché. Once full they will need to be cut open to get at the money!

FOLDED PAPER

Origami

Paper folding is a useful skill to learn. Follow the instructions and once you have mastered them, if you have a sheet of paper, you will never be without a box. Use stiff card to make a large box and small sheets of paper to make a smaller one. Origami boxes can be used to store party favours, sweets, wedding confetti and odds and ends. A sturdy, card-folded box could be used as a simple tray to hold biscuits. Have a go, all you need is a sheet of paper and a little practice.

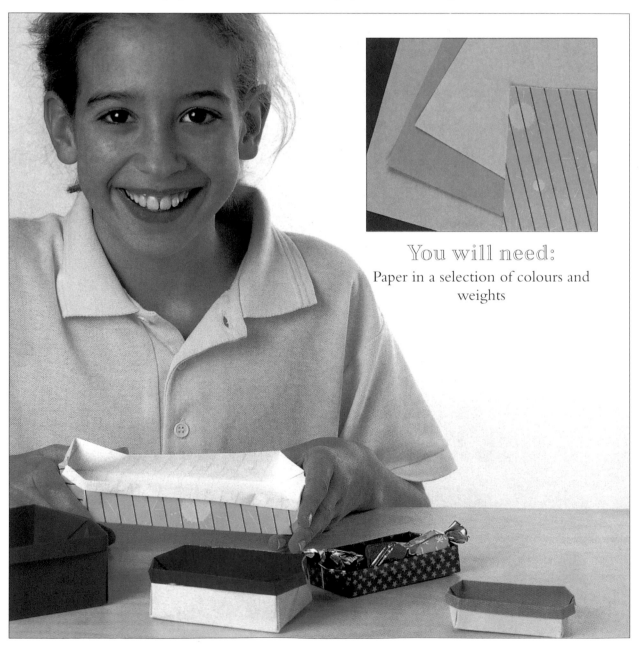

You will need:

Paper in a selection of colours and weights

1 Fold the paper in half lengthways.

2 Fold each half into the middle.

3 Make a small fold back outwards on both sides.

4 Fold in the corners and tuck them under the small fold.

5 Place your fingers in the corners and lift the box into shape.

When paper folding, be sure to press the folds firmly so they are sharp.

GIFTS, CARDS AND DECORATIONS
Easter

In the Northern hemisphere Easter occurs in the springtime, so we have Easter bunnies, eggs and spring flowers, such as the daffodils on this delightful Easter card. It is fun to make and grandparents will enjoy receiving greeting cards at this time of year. The chocolate nests are made from breakfast cereal and melted chocolate. The tiny eggs are chocolate covered raisins, or, instead, you could use small foil covered chocolate Easter eggs. Another fun Easter activity is to make an Easter tree. This tree is made from a branch and decorated with paper Easter eggs.

You will need:

Shredded breakfast cereal

Bowl

Melted chocolate

Spoon

Foil

Bun tin

Chocolate covered raisins

1 Crumble the cereal by hand into a bowl. Check that there are no large chunks.

2 Carefully add the melted chocolate to the bowl of crumbled cereal and, using the spoon, mix well together.

3 Line a bun tin with foil and place a spoonful of the mixture into each space. Use the back of the spoon to press it down into a nest shape. Leave the shapes to harden in a cool, dry place.

4 When the nests are hard, put them on a plate and add a few chocolate covered raisins to each one. Serve up at tea time on Easter Sunday.

5 A branch decorated with paper Easter eggs will brighten up the home. Cut the Easter eggs from paper and decorate them using pencil crayons. Make a hole at one end of each egg and thread with string to hang them on the Easter tree.

6 Use coloured paper to make this Easter card. The daffodils have bright yellow paper petals and a paler yellow centre. Cut the leaves from green paper. Use glue to attach the flowers to the card.

SAND AND PETAL PICTURE
Diwali

Followers of the Hindu religion celebrate many festivals. Diwali or the Festival of Light is my favourite Hindu festival. Diwali is celebrated around October/November time and is a New Year celebration. In Hindu homes the house is cleaned and decorated with coloured glitter, sand and flowers. Lots of small clay lamps are kept burning on windowsills and on doorsteps. These lights are to welcome Lakshmi, the goddess of wealth. Everyone hopes she will visit them over this period and bring good fortune for the New Year. Many Hindu homes in India have sand pictures drawn up outside their front doors to welcome visitors.

Make a sand and flower picture to place in your hall during Diwali.

You will need:
Air hardening clay

Paint-brush and paint

Paper and pencil

Glue stick

Coloured sand

Flower petals

Glitter

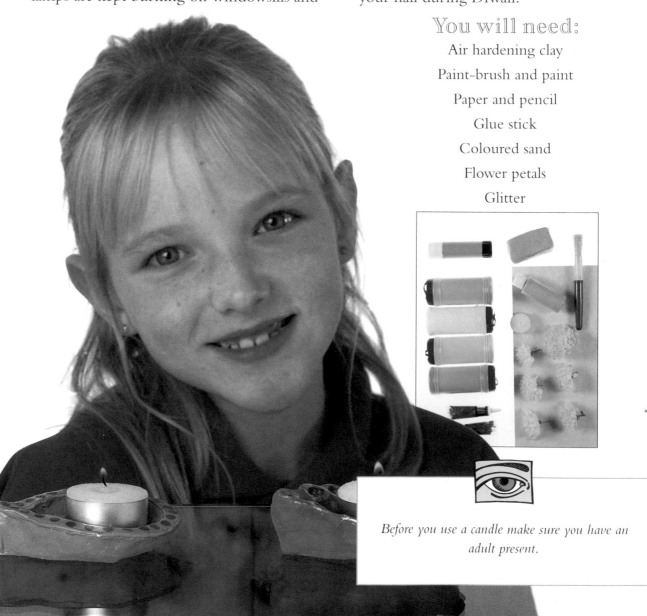

Before you use a candle make sure you have an adult present.

1 To make your Diwali lamp you will need a ball of air hardening clay. Use your fingers to shape it into a bowl shape and press a fancy edge into the clay. When the lamp has dried, paint it in bright colours and decorate with gold or silver paint. Place a nightlight candle in the lamp and check with an adult before you light it.

2 You will need a large piece of paper. Use a pencil to sketch a flower picture onto the paper. Use a glue stick to mark the centre of the flower.

3 Pour coloured sand onto the glue mark.

4 Next use the glue stick to mark out the shape of the petals.

5 Pour coloured sand onto the glue lines.

6 When you have completed the sand picture place flower petals as a border.

8 Use glitter to add the finishing touch to your Diwali picture.

Measurements

TEMPERATURE

Fahrenheit	Centigrade
250–300	120–150
300–350	150–175
350–375	175–190
375–400	190–200
400–425	200–220

LENGTH

cm	ins
2.5	1
5	2
7.6	3
10	4
12.7	5
15	6
17.7	7
20	8
22.8	9
25.4	10

WEIGHT

oz	grams
1	30
3	75
6	175
8	250